Tiptoe Into Scary Places

Deserted Cities

by E. Merwin

Consultant: Ursula Bielski
Author and Paranormal Researcher
Founder of Chicago Hauntings, Inc.

Bearport Publishing
New York, New York

Credits
Cover, © Ewais/Shutterstock; TOC, © Taras Kolomiyets/Shutterstock; 4–5, © Jose Gregorio/Shutterstock and © dezi/Shutterstock; 6L, © Mainichi Shimbun/Reuters; 6R, © Robert Gilhooly/Alamy Stock Photo; 7, © ZUMA Press, Inc./Alamy Stock Photo; 8, © Tupungato/Shutterstock, © elwynn/Shutterstock, and © Top Photo Engineer/Shutterstock; 9, © ZUMA Press, Inc./Alamy Stock Photo, © szefei/Shutterstock, © Top Photo Engineer/Shutterstock, © kimberrywood/Shutterstock, and © Photobac/Shutterstock; 10L, © 2017 Google Map Data; 10R, © reivax/CC BY-SA 4.0; 11, © Mary Evans Picture Library/Alamy Stock Photo; 12, © Christopher Payne/ESTO; 13, © Photo Researchers, Inc/Alamy Stock Photo; 14, William M. Harmer/Public Domain; 15, © Yoho 2001/CC BY-SA 3.0; 16, © Maria Legault; 17, © f11photo/Shutterstock and © Donna Beeler/Shutterstock; 18L, © North Wind Picture Archives/Alamy Stock Photo; 18R, © Gary Saxe/Shutterstock; 19, © Paul Briden/Shutterstock and © Potapov Alexander/Shutterstock; 20L, © Sue Leonard Photography/Shutterstock; 20R, © JesseChilders/Shutterstock, and © CREATISTA/Shutterstock; 21, © Russ Bishop/Alamy Stock Photo; 23, © Sergey Kamshylin/Shutterstock; 24, © Fotokon/Shutterstock.

Publisher: Kenn Goin
Editor: Jessica Rudolph
Creative Director: Spencer Brinker
Photo Researcher: Thomas Persano
Cover: Kim Jones

Library of Congress Cataloging-in-Publication Data in process at time of publication (2018)
Library of Congress Control Number: 2017005329
ISBN-13: 978-1-68402-269-4 (library binding)

For more information, write to Bearport Publishing Company, Inc., 45 West 21st Street, Suite 3B, New York, New York 10010. Printed in the United States of America.

10 9 8 7 6 5 4 3 2 1

Contents

Deserted Cities

You walk through an old, **abandoned** city that was once filled with people. The crumbling buildings have been taken over by weeds. As you turn a corner, you hear a faint rustling sound. Then you start to feel as if someone's staring at you. You look around, but no one's there! Is it possible the **spirits** of the past still lurk in the shadows?

Get ready to read four terrifying tales about **deserted** cities. Turn the page . . . if you have the nerve!

Disaster in Japan

Fukushima, Japan

In March 2011, an **earthquake** rocked Japan. It caused a giant 132-foot (40 m) wave called a **tsunami** to rise out of the ocean. More than 15,000 people drowned.

The tsunami hitting land

A destroyed home

No one knows the **fate** of 2,600 people who are still missing. They could have drowned in the flood or been crushed in the earthquake. But while they are thought to be dead, their restless spirits may still roam the streets.

The summer after the disaster, taxi drivers near Fukushima reported picking up peculiar passengers. One driver said a young woman wanted to go to a deserted part of the city. He told her the city was empty, and she asked, "Have I died?" When the driver turned around, the backseat was empty!

Other ghosts have been seen outside abandoned shops in Fukushima. Many are missing limbs. Some are even headless!

Island of Death

North Brother Island, New York City

There's a part of New York City that's been abandoned for more than 50 years. Few people dare to visit this creepy place. Why?

North Brother Island has a dark history. In 1904, a boat carrying many people caught on fire and sank.

North Brother Island

An abandoned hospital

Some people burned in the flames, while others drowned. **Tragically,** more than 1,000 people died. Many bodies washed ashore on North Brother Island.

The island's gloomy past also includes a hospital that treated patients with **tuberculosis.** People with this disease coughed up blood and wasted away in terrible pain. They died in the hospital, never to return home.

The tuberculosis hospital

The island's most famous resident was Mary Mallon, also known as **Typhoid** Mary. As a cook in New York City, she spread typhoid to 57 people. In 1915, to stop her from spreading the disease, she was forced to live on North Brother Island.

Mary Mallon with other patients on North Brother Island

The Girl Who Stayed

Indiana, Ontario, Canada

About 150 years ago, Indiana, Ontario, was a busy town. Many people worked at the **sawmills** that shipped lumber down the Grand River. When a railroad was built to transport lumber more quickly, it didn't reach Indiana. The town was doomed.

Within a few years, the workers found jobs in other towns.

Lumberjacks

Over time, their wooden houses rotted away. At the heart of this ghost town, only the Thompson mansion still stands. With its nearby family graveyard, the home is a spooky place to visit.

The Thompson mansion

In the 1800s, young Bessie Thompson lived in the mansion and played on the grounds. But when she became ill, she couldn't leave the house. She often sat on the stairs looking out the front entrance. Sadly, she died of **diphtheria** at age ten.

Today, some visitors say they feel a mysterious force as they walk through the family graveyard. Others claim to have seen a ghostly girl sitting on the staircase in the mansion.

There are no photographs of Bessie, but in an old letter, her father described his daughter. The description matches what visitors have said about the ghostly girl more than 100 years later!

THE CURSE OF BODIE

Bodie, California

In the 1870s, a miner discovered gold in eastern California. There, a busy town with stores, hotels, and saloons popped up. Over the years, miners found less and less gold and moved away. Then several fires destroyed Bodie.

Gold miners

Bodie

One fire was started by a boy who didn't get a cake for his birthday! He set fire to his kitchen table, and the spreading flames destroyed more than half the town. Today, no one lives in Bodie, but **park rangers** have reported ghostly encounters.

In the abandoned buildings, lights turn on by themselves, and mysterious voices sing. In one house, a ghostly maid is seen in the window.

Some people believe these spirits protect the town from thieves. They say there is a **curse**, and whoever steals from Bodie will experience terrible things.

In fact, many visitors send back items they've stolen, along with letters apologizing to Bodie's spirits!

A visitor to Bodie saw his daughter playing with an invisible friend. Then he noticed a nearby tombstone that belonged to Evelyn Myers, who died in 1897 at age three. Was the daughter playing with Evelyn's ghost?

Deserted Cities Around the World

Bodie
California

Explore the not-so-deserted buildings of this ghost town.

Indiana
Ontario, Canada

Visit this town and a lonely girl from its past.

North Brother Island
New York City

Discover a secret island and share its deadly history!

Fukushima
Japan

Tour the ghostly areas of this abandoned city.

Glossary

abandoned (uh-BAN-duhnd) left empty and without care

curse (KURS) something that causes evil or injury

deserted (duh-ZUR-tid) having no people living in an area

diphtheria (dip-THEER-ee-uh) a sickness that makes breathing very difficult

earthquake (URTH-kwayk) a sudden shaking of the ground caused by the moving of Earth's outer layer

fate (FAYT) final result

park rangers (PARK RAYN-jurz) workers in charge of protecting parklands

sawmills (SAW-milz) places where trees are cut into lumber

spirits (SPIHR-its) supernatural creatures, such as ghosts

tragically (TRAJ-ik-lee) very sadly or unfortunately

tsunami (tsoo-NAH-mee) a huge ocean wave or group of waves caused by an earthquake

tuberculosis (too-*bur*-kyuh-LOH-sis) a serious disease that damages the lungs

typhoid (TYE-foyd) a disease that causes a high fever and can be deadly

Index

Read More

Rocklin, Joanne. *This Book Is Haunted (An I Can Read Book).* New York: HarperCollins (2002).

Teitelbaum, Michael. *Terror at the Ghost Town Mine (Cold Whispers).* New York: Bearport (2016).

Learn More Online

To learn more about deserted cities, visit:
www.bearportpublishing.com/Tiptoe

About the Author

E. Merwin wanted a beagle for her seventh birthday but got a typewriter instead. She has been writing ever since.